Our American Ethos

Our American Ethos

◆

Renewing Our Trust and Belief in America

Jason M. Ritchie

iUniverse, Inc.
New York Lincoln Shanghai

Our American Ethos
Renewing Our Trust and Belief in America

iUniverse books may be ordered through booksellers or by contacting:

iUniverse
2021 Pine Lake Road, Suite 100
Lincoln, NE 68512
www.iuniverse.com
1-800-Authors (1-800-288-4677)

ISBN-13: 978-0-595-36725-2 (pbk)
ISBN-13: 978-0-595-81146-5 (ebk)
ISBN-10: 0-595-36725-9 (pbk)
ISBN-10: 0-595-81146-9 (ebk)

Printed in the United States of America

It is time to renew our trust and belief in representative government and in each other as fellow citizens. This is the goal of the American Ethos.

American Ethos is the common bond we share as Americans. It defines who we are as a nation and a people. American Ethos is the recognition that we are citizens of the greatest country in the world, blessed with constitutionally-mandated rights, opportunities and obligations that are ours to protect and defend. It is a spirit of unity and commonality. American Ethos binds our varied and often conflicting individual interests together into common responsibility, mutual respect and a shared vision of our American future.

American Ethos is the acknowledgment that although we live in different regions and communities of our great land and we share diverse political perspectives, ethnic backgrounds and religious persuasions, it is more important to view ourselves as Americans—sharing common freedoms and a common future, confronting challenges as a unified nation. It is the goal of the American Ethos to emphasize and nurture the unifying qualities and not single out our individual priorities.

American Ethos is the opposite of partisanship. It is the recognition that blindly following the mutually exclusive partisan values of Democrats and Republicans is not unifying; it is overtly divisive and damaging to our common American future. American Ethos calls for independent thinking and open questioning of authority. It demands accountable and responsible leadership that brings us together as a nation. It requires shared responsibility for our country and our collective future—that we take an American perspective on our American issues.

American Ethos is the idea that the achievement of mutually beneficial goals is the best way to grow our national unity and ensure our future as a free and democratic America. It is the prospect that we can establish basic ideals we all share as Americans—not based on a particular social value, special interest, partisan or local concern, but rather by looking at our country and our people as a whole group, not a collection of competing minorities.

American Ethos means understanding and cultivating the idea that we are owner-operators of America—that regardless of our political party preference, whatever our religion, race or gender, as American citizens we share a fundamental duty: to make our government meet our needs—to make our government work with us, not against us—to preserve, protect and defend our country and our freedoms for generations to come.

Our American democracy demands its citizens serve as active and progressive owner-operators of our representative government. We cannot sit back and hope that others will do the right thing. It is up to us as Americans to protect our American Constitution and our fellow citizens with eternal vigilance from both external and internal threats. For our American way of life to endure, we must recognize that our representative government requires hands-on participation by its citizens.

I believe that we, as American owner-operators of our representative government, have collectively lost control—we have lost our American Ethos. We have failed to defend our rights and our freedoms. We have allowed divisive values, extreme partisanship and radical special interest groups that are intent on manipulating the system to their own ends to take over. The political discourse in America—the ongoing conversation between all Americans over the issues that affect all of us—has become so rancorous and so partisan that our representative democracy is failing. We have lost sight of common American ideals and have taken on the false mantels of regionalism and reactionism to cloak our lost faith in American Democracy. This must change and it is up to us to change it.

American Ethos is the belief that we can change our nation, our government and our political system for the benefit of all Americans—not for the very few but for the many. This is the goal of the American Ethos: to bring us together around commonly held basic American ideals—not religious or partisan values but *American* ideals—to create a better government and country in order to ensure that future Americans are able to enjoy the same rights, opportunities and obligations we have and more.

◆   ◆   ◆

The concept of an American Ethos is not new. Unity of spirit and commonality of purpose have shown themselves throughout our history. Understanding what an American Ethos can be today requires understanding our history and learning from our past.

We have so much to be proud of in our more than 225 year history; as a people and a nation. In comparison with any other country in the history of the world, no one can claim our level of accomplishments in such a short history. We have become the beacon of hope for the hopeless from around the world. We have proven that government by the people and for the people can thrive. We have saved the world from Nazism and Communism and we have walked on the Moon. We are, without a doubt, a nation without equal in history.

There have been and there will be times in our history when generations of Americans are asked to step forward and accept responsibility for their future and the future of all Americans. Now is one of those times.

When I think of American Ethos in American history, I think of the Progressive Era in the early 1900's, when Americans came together to oust corrupt politicians that were being manipulated by wealthy industrialists. Americans across social and political lines stood up and demanded changes in their government. A wave of pride swept across America that reclaimed basic American ideals of account-ability and fairness. Dishonest politicians were removed and Americans reclaimed ownership of their governments at all levels: local, state and federal. This did not solve everything. The issues that divided Americans remained, but the process of dealing with those issues was no longer tainted by the interests of the wealthy and powerful. The voices of the American people could be heard without the over-whelming and corrupting power of money and influence blocking their way. The Progressive Era in America demonstrated how we can unify as a nation and reclaim ownership of our country.

I recall the efforts made by Americans in the 1930's during the Great Depression and 1940's during World War II. Americans invested in themselves and their country by making sacrifices toward a greater goal. Common threats and needs were recognized and acted on with unanimity of spirit. When the economy col-lapsed into the Great Depression, Americans went to work rebuilding the Ameri-can infrastructure. They took jobs and filled needs in every field, all the time working for a greater, common good. When we were attacked and brought into

World War II, Americans acted to defend their country by enlisting into the military and working in war industries. They did their part as individuals, recognizing that their contribution was at the same time essential for themselves and their families, but also for Americans they had never met.

These generations of Americans met the challenges of their time by recognizing threats to America, both internal and external, and acting with a unified purpose and shared responsibility. We can and must do it again. This is the goal of the America Ethos.

◆   ◆   ◆

What happened to our American unity? What is causing us to be so alienated from each other? The answer is that the dividing forces of marginalizing values, extreme partisanship, and unchecked special interest groups have colluded to become poison to our government and our society.

America today is a house divided, split right down the middle between conservative Republican and liberal Democrat. We have become a hyper-partisan nation, more concerned with imposing our moral view on each other than protecting our shared rights and common future. The issues that divide us—those wedge issues that cause us to fall into separate and opposing camps—are being co-opted and dominated by partisan extremists and religious zealots that manipulate facts and breed intolerance, fear and division. For too long, we have failed to recognize and utilize our unique American diversity and the strength that this variety brings to our common future. Instead, we allow ourselves to be distracted, divided and dominated.

The problems we confront as a nation are not being solved. They are encouraged as a means to marginalize and manipulate us into controllable groups. We have become individualists, defending our own interests and values, with no regard for our fellow countrymen. We have become slaves to our selfish wants and pawns of narrow-minded interest groups that have hijacked our Government with unregulated and free-flowing money. Our federal government, reflective of its most radical constituents, has become a pointless debating society where gridlock, obstructionism and personal attacks are the rules of combat. Liberal and conservative extremes are the only voices heard. Our elected officials are concerned with only the most wealthy and politically-connected Americans. The voice of the common American is ignored by partisan leaders while their special interest handlers espouse values that are mutually exclusive and overtly divisive.

Our divided nation confronts a self-destructive culture war whereby the moral and religious convictions of a vocal and boisterous minority are being forced upon all Americans. Our nation is being torn apart by these zealots in the name of their narrow and intolerant definition of progress. These fellow Americans believe that America has seen its best day. They want to restore our country to its past glory by politicizing traditional values and cultural separators, thereby forcing a condescending and arrogant point of view on all Americans. These so-called values are based on close-minded religious doctrine that is neither American nor unifying. In order for these fear-based traditional values to take hold, Americans are made to hate and fear each other, emphasizing the dissimilarities and variations that make all Americans unique. We simply cannot tolerate the subversion and politicizing of morals and values by those that seek to impose their personal judgments upon everyone. It is simply un-American.

American Ethos is the recognition that it is our shared obligation to be constantly vigilant of any partisan judgments, political perspectives or moral declarations that claim to be morally and ethically superior to the exclusion of all others. This vigilance means we must learn to distinguish between the valuable qualities that religious and cultural identification can bring to a free and open society versus the misuse of religion and traditional values as weapons to distract, divide and dominate.

American Ethos demands the rejection of traditional and religious values as tools to dismantle and manipulate our American democracy. Our constitutionally protected right to practice our chosen religion must not become a dividing factor between us as Americans. We are a multi-cultural, multi-religious society where mutual respect must prevail. It is our shared freedom to practice religion, to build values and cultural ties—these freedoms are what make us American. These freedoms must be reinforced and protected, not diminished and co-opted into the weapons of an 'us versus them' society.

American Ethos is based on the idea that it is our unique qualities—our individual distinction—that is our shared American strength. America Ethos is the notion that every opinion, every religion, every value has validity and legitimacy in America, because in America, no single opinion, religion or value has more importance than another. Every voice is equal and has the right to be heard, because in America, freedom of speech, freedom of religion and freedom of expression are as sacred as the air we breathe. American Ethos is the recognition that it is our shared freedoms and our common interest in the preservation of our rights that makes us American.

American Ethos requires that Americans make a choice: are we defined by our individual culture and values or by our shared freedoms and citizenship? American Ethos is the belief that it is our common freedoms and our shared citizenship in the greatest country in the world that is our common bond as Americans. From our shared American citizenship come our unique American freedoms: the freedom to choose to whom we pray, with whom we associate and how we live our lives. These shared freedoms must be protected.

Our unique American freedoms will become meaningless and we will have no common future as a nation if we continue to devolve into sectarian and cultural division. Our shared American future demands that we do not allow our individual religious or cultural identification to dictate our politics and our social discourse. American Ethos is about recognizing that we are a country of varied and diverse nationalities, cultures and religions, all equal to each other and with a common future, a common future that must supersede our individual moral and value-based judgments against each other.

◆   ◆   ◆

Building our national unity is not a simple prospect. Everyday our partisan political leaders and their special interest handlers breed fear and factionalism. We are separated by those who seek to control the political power of our representative democracy. Special interest groups, with their own agendas, their own narrow views as to how our government and our society should operate, have the ear of our elected officials. They have bought their way into power and influence using the politics of hate and division. They use tools such as the partisan media and complicit election laws to breed the separation and manipulation that allows them to control our government.

Every day we are subdivided, classified and regionalized into controllable groups. We are made to feel we share nothing in common with our fellow Americans. We are fighting against each other: Red States versus Blue States, liberal coasts versus conservative middle America, urban industrialized north versus the agricultural rural south. The notion of a shared American future is not part of our collective political consciousness because it is not in the interests of the extreme partisan leaders of our nation to build American unity. They can only maintain power when they keep us in fear of each other.

Americans today confront fanatic and divisive "political commentarians" posing as legitimate sources of unbiased news and information. In reality, these "political commntarians" are spewing the lies and mistruths of special interests and extreme partisanship. Whether on talk radio, in newspaper editorials or on cable news channels, the culture of extremist perspectives and partisan commentary plays fast and loose with the truth. Their truth is perspective. They are more concerned with swaying public and political opinion than with accuracy or truth. They play to an audience that is easily manipulated and alienated from its American roots. Their ideologically-based commentary is spoken and received as divinely inspired truth, when in reality it is at best, partisan opinion and at worst, morally repugnant and manipulative lies.

Partisan extremist propaganda, from both Democrats and Republicans, causes us to be divided as a nation and a people. Instead of building a common vision of the future, where everyone has a vested interest, they have created an empty society without trust and mutual respect. We are fighting each other, protecting little and achieving nothing. This cannot stand.

America Ethos is the recognition that we are a country of multiple and competing beliefs and interests and that a representative government with built-in checks and balances is, by design, in constant flux between those competing belief and interests. However, the situation has devolved to the point where the entire system has failed to react to the needs of the American people as a whole. The politics of personal destruction and extreme partisanship have derailed our government, turning American against American.

When divisive values, corrupting partisanship and isolating special interest groups overwhelm our American political conversation—when uncompromising ideology, manipulation and distrust have become the rule, not the exception—it is easy to see why our government and our society are so divided and at the breaking point. This is not the way things are supposed to be. We simply cannot stand for a system that allows partisan extremists to rule our government, protecting their limited interests, while those of us in the middle, the silent majority, dream of a better America not knowing how to act.

The fact is, all of this is our responsibility but we have collectively failed to defend our country. We have lost our American identity and have become a fear-based society. We have lost faith in our government and in ourselves as a people. We are neither owners nor operators of our America. This must change—now.

◆   ◆   ◆

Taking back ownership of America demands defending our shared American ideals. Not your values or my values, not religious or moral values, not ideological or partisan values but our shared American ideals. American Ethos is the restoration of our American ownership, our trust and respect for each other as Americans through mutual beneficial action.

To restore our American Ethos, we must focus our efforts on measures that make this a better place for all Americans, not a powerful few. We must oust the corrupt and divisive and reestablish our national identity. We must set out American priorities that are mutually agreed upon and commonly beneficial for all Americans. For example, I believe that this is a shared American priority we can all agree upon: As Americans, we are obligated to live in such a way as to make this America a better one than we found. Whether we are conservative or liberal, urban or rural, we are Americans first, and can agree on the simple idea of wanting to leave a better country with more opportunities for those Americans who come after us. I believe this is something we all share as Americans. This is American Ethos.

American Ethos means fighting against the power and influence of value dividers, wealthy special interest groups, extreme partisanship and the impact these forces have on our national spirit. We must fight the temptation to go to the radical edges of our society. We must seek commonality between us as Americans. We must come together and not be driven apart. We must fight for our freedom every day by exercising our rights to speak out, to vote and to change the system to meet our common American needs. This is American Ethos.

America Ethos is the recognition that it is the responsibility of our elected leaders to bring us together by setting goals that are of benefit to all. A balance between left and right must be found, a balance that must serve the greater good by achieving goals that are progressive and communally beneficial. If our leaders fail to act as unifiers, then we must lead for them by demanding action to restore our trust in each other, as a nation and as a people. It is our shared responsibility and our common obligation under our representative government and our democratic constitution to serve as citizen leaders and to enact change to better our nation. We must accept our shared obligation to move beyond the distraction and division. This is real ownership of America. This is American Ethos.

Through working together toward commonly held American goals, we can rebuild the trust and respect that is the basis of American democracy and the foundation of the American Ethos. We must take some initial steps together, based on commonly held American priorities and without the yoke of the corruptors and dividers. We must deal with basic American needs first. Based on this achievement, we will gain the confidence, trust and mutual respect to move forward and address the difficult issues that confront us. This is American Ethos.

◆   ◆   ◆

As Americans, we have so much in common, so much we can agree upon. What is stopping us from moving forward on commonly held American priorities? There will always be those that are slaves to their particular regional, moral or special interest, those that are only responsive to fear, hate and money. Are we destined to let the moral manipulators, partisan extremists and special interests corrupt the system simply because we choose not to organize ourselves into a unified power under a common American spirit? Those dividing forces are hoping for just that so they can maintain their hold on power. If we do not act now, we will only have ourselves to blame as we continue to fester in this morass of gridlock and partisan warfare that drags us from left to right—making no forward progress.

I believe the time to act is now. I am an American just like you and I want ownership of my country back. I am tried of being out of control, watching professional politicians and their special interest handlers drive our nation into isolated groups. That we have lost our unity, lost our common American idealism—this makes me want to stand up and reclaim our American Ethos. If we can simply agree that building a unified nation through the achievement of mutually beneficial goals is the best way to ensure a free and prosperous America in the future, I believe we can succeed.

What I am proposing is a revolution in our society and our government—a new start, a new direction for our nation to cultivate an American Ethos. We simply cannot tolerate a system where our elected officials are beholden to partisan interests and limited religious values, serving only the few. We must reclaim our government in the name of progressive American idealism. We must set commonly held, mutually beneficial priorities that the majority will support and elect representatives that will act in the American best interest. We must move forward as a unified nation if we are going to move forward at all. Through our new genuine unity, we can grow together as a people and as a country, guaranteeing our future as a free and democratic America for generations to come.

This is the goal of the American Ethos.

◆   ◆   ◆

American Ethos Platform

The idea behind American Ethos is simply that we can do so much more good for ourselves and our children if we find the certain tangible things we essentially agree upon as Americans and then begin to work together to regain our trust in each other. This is not to say we all want the same things—just that we can set out certain commonly held priorities and beliefs that we as Americans share and that these can be the foundation of a new American unity. I believe these commonly held beliefs can be summarized in this phrase:

As Americans, we want to live in a safe land with the protections of our Constitution, while having the opportunity to get good jobs and protecting the same opportunities for our children.

This principle is the foundation of the American Ethos platform. I believe that the federal government should act through the mechanism of the legislative process, in conjunction with state and local governments, commercial businesses and the public, to perpetuate this principle.

The American Ethos Platform has 3 primary functions:

Defense of the American Homeland and Constitution
Perpetual Creation of Jobs
Universal Education

These 3 functions represent the most democratic and pluralist ideals in America. No matter where you live, what you do, whether you are Democrat or Republican, we can all agree on these basic functions. They are basic American needs, not ideological or political beliefs. Making common American needs a priority is an essential concept in the American Ethos platform. When we gain freedom from extremism, partisanship and divisive special interests to create a better way of life for all Americans, all Americans gain strength, our democracy gains strength and we become true owner-operators of our government and our future.

We can build a unified and progressive America if we recognize it is our common responsibility and our shared obligation to address common needs, enact legislation that finds a balance between public and private responsibility, allocate resources from all levels of government, and follow through on implementation as if our future depends on it—because it does. This is true ownership of our nation and our future.

What follows is a platform of ideas and proposals that reflect the shared principles and ideals of the American Ethos. This platform strives to balance the needs of all sides by serving the greater good for all Americans. The goal behind all of these proposals and the American Ethos is to build social unity through mutually beneficial achievement—to bring us together as a nation and a people by building common bonds, so that we can be assured of a future for Americans yet to come.

<u>Defense of the American Homeland and Constitution</u>

1. *American Civil Defense*
2. *Automobile Renewable Resources Commitment*
3. *100% American Defense Procurement*
4. *Removal of Weapons of Mass Destruction*
5. *Global AIDS Treatment and Eradication*
6. *Foreign Financial Aid Reform*
7. *Legalization for Qualified Undocumented Workers*

8. *Federal Voting Standards and Procedures*
9. *Federal Election Holiday*

Perpetual Creation of Jobs

1. *Infrastructure Reinvestment*
2. *Job Creation through Tax Incentives*
3. *National Service Consolidation; American Community Corps*
4. *Outsourcing Moratorium*
5. *Trade Expansion and Intellectual Property Protection*
6. *Research and Development Initiative*

Universal Education

1. *New Schools Program*
2. *National Education Standards and Testing*
3. *The TVCC Program*
4. *Science and Technology Education Initiative*
5. *Continuing Education for Instructors*

◆   ◆   ◆

Defense of the American Homeland and Constitution

The defense of our American homeland and our American Constitution must be our primary responsibility. Everything else about our shared future, all other considerations derive from our essential need to live in a safe land with the protections of our American Constitution. It is essential to the growth of our freedoms, our civil rights and civil liberties, that we live in a safe land, free from foreign threats. Our constitutional rights go hand in hand with a defended homeland. The two are inseparable.

I believe that it is the direct responsibility of our elected officials and our federal government to protect our homeland and our constitutional rights. As Americans, we must unify and direct our representative government to utilize any and all available means to defend against terrorists, belligerent foreign states and any efforts to undermine our democracy and constitutional freedoms. Partisanship and politics cannot be allowed to interfere. Our common security and freedoms are too important. Proactive measures to ensure our democracy, our peace and our safety are essential to our American democracy and the American Ethos.

◆   ◆   ◆

We must work to build an American Ethos in our foreign relations that will serve to improve the place we hold in the world. We must strive to achieve peace, harmony and mutual respect with our neighbors, while achieving unity and progress at home. Whether we engage in trade or defense treaties, diplomatic relationships or international community membership, I believe that the defense of our American homeland must be the most important concern.

To create a safe homeland, we must build relationships based on trade, commerce and respect where each country can benefit mutually. We must build cultural and diplomatic ties so that we can better understand regional and local interests as well as the religions and customs of the peoples of the world. When we better understand the unique qualities of each nation and people of the world, when we create shared interests, we can build mutual respect and better formulate effective foreign policy that defends our American homeland. America's first line of defense must be through our global engagement on all levels.

I believe we should foster an American Ethos internally and domestically, but I do not believe we should spread its principles to the four corners of the world. We have a great thing going here in America and cultivating an American Ethos is our effort to make it even better. Building an American Ethos should only improve our respect for our institutions, obligations and opportunities unique to America. That does not mean we should subvert the development of foreign nations by demanding they conform to our point of view.

While I firmly believe that democracy and freedom of expression are essential to an open society and the foundation of the American Ethos, that does not necessarily mean that every culture, religion or nation in the world want the same thing. We cannot assume the rest of the world wants our way of life. We should respect other peoples and countries by not insisting on the supremacy of our world view, thereby overwhelming other legitimate perspectives. What works for us may not work for everyone else. We must allow the natural political evolution that occurred here in America to occur in foreign nations without American manipulation and influence.

There are times when America must step in diplomatically, economically and militarily to prevent the mass loss of human life and the destabilization of a foreign country. This is a responsibility we simply must meet. Where there is hunger in the world, we must act. Where there is disease, we must act. Where our diplomatic or trading relationships would preserve peace, we must act. Where human rights are threatened, we must act. We must act as a responsible member of the world community—as a leader when necessary, but always as an active participant in the concern of peace. Where we can act with other nations and multinational organizations to remedy global issues, we must act as a partnership. Above all, when America itself is in any way threatened, we must not hesitate to act.

There have been and will continue to be global crises and threats to America. When the American homeland and its citizens are threatened, we must act decisively to not only neutralize the threat, but to send a message of future consequences. We will not be made to live terrorized by any foreign threat. We will deal with any threat against our country with as much force as we deem necessary to secure our homeland and citizenry.

When it comes to military force, I believe we should utilize the doctrine coined by former Secretary of State Colin Powell. The Powell Doctrine states that military action should only be used as a last resort and only if there is a clear and obvious threat to our national security. The doctrine states that the military force, when used, should be overwhelming and disproportionate to the force used by the enemy. Additionally, there must be strong support for the action by the American public with a clear exit strategy from the conflict. I believe this doctrine meets the goals of our American Ethos and the defense of our homeland.

When we act to defend our American homeland, it is essential that our actions are understood and respected or we risk breeding global animosity. I believe that it continues to be in our best interests to find, document and make public evidence of aggressive foreign powers. We must be able to identify, document and confront threats abroad before they become security threats to the American homeland. We must demand vigorous intelligence gathering and analysis from our federal government and our law enforcement agencies. When threats to America are found and when action is necessary, we must confront any and all threats to America and defend our action in the name of the defense of America and its citizenry.

◆   ◆   ◆

The defense of our American homeland through progressive actions throughout the globe is essential to our freedom and our democracy and the goal of the America Ethos. Equally as important as the defense of our homeland is our shared obligation to reinforce our American democracy at home through progressive and mutually beneficial actions.

Building faith into our electoral process and into our elected officials is essential to our democracy and a vital part of cultivating our American Ethos. We cannot hope to instill trust in our representative government and build a common future if we do not treat our obligation to vote with the dignity it deserves.

American Ethos demands the American citizenry to wrestle back control of our government from extremism, partisanship and special interests. Our Constitutional obligation to vote is our most potent weapon to win this battle. Our right to vote must be reinforced, protected and above all utilized. How we vote, the care with which we vote—the accuracy, the legitimacy, the reverence of this quintessentially democratic act—the way in which we practice our democracy must be our gift to future generations of Americans.

As Americans, we confront an electoral process that has devolved into an untrustworthy mass of procedural inconsistencies in which millions of Americans are disenfranchised. We have lost control of our American democracy. We have allowed extremism, too much money and too much special interest influence into our election system—the result being dangerously low voter turnout by our fellow citizens and increasing apathy for our common future. This cannot stand. We must take action to protect our democracy and our future as a nation.

Our right to vote is our shared American responsibility—it is our American Ethos. All of our other Constitutional rights derive from this essential obligation. We must act now to give our elections more authority and legitimacy. We must demand elections that are procedurally consistent state by state, with results we can trust. We must demand transparency, openness and the ability to make informed decisions in the voting booth. We must guarantee that our right to vote be elevated to the status it deserves. The America I believe in deserves no less.

American Ethos is the belief in a strong and unified America, one where we can live in harmony with the international community and enjoy the privileges and responsibilities of American citizenship. It is the duty of our federal government to assure our future peace and prosperity by taking proactive steps that protect our constitutional rights and our homeland.

◆   ◆   ◆

American Civil Defense

It is our shared responsibility to defend our American homeland. Our National Guard and our Coast Guard, our last line of defense in the protection of our American homeland, must not be distracted and diverted into overseas commitments. These forces will form the backbone of our American Civil Defense force.

I believe that it is the solemn responsibility of our federal government and our citizenry to protect and defend the American homeland from any and all threats. This responsibility is an essential component to the peace and security of the American Ethos. For our national unity to thrive, we must feel safe in our homeland but also be prepared to deal with aggression on our shores. As Americans, we must unite and insist that our citizenry, our cities and towns, our infrastructure and natural resources are protected from and prepared for aggression in our homeland.

American Ethos demands that all resources and available measures be utilized to prepare for enemies that will inevitably continue to attempt to bring terror and destruction to the American homeland. Failures in security of the past must never be repeated. We know they are coming. We must be prepared—there are no excuses.

I propose the creation of a consolidated civil defense force, under the authority of the Department of Homeland Security, that will have one purpose—to utilize all available technology and manpower to protect and defend the American homeland from terrorism and internal security threats. Through the direction of the Department of Homeland Security, our American Civil Defense force will proactively prepare, defend, reinforce and secure our American homeland. As Americans, we must insure that our last line of defense, our homeland—our borders, our seaports and airports, our cities and towns—are secure from foreign threats.

The American Civil Defense force will utilize our National Guard and our Coast Guard to form a flexible force that will be able to react to internal security needs. Our American Civil Defense force will incorporate our Air Marshal program with airport, seaport and border security. Our local and state police forces, our local fire departments and our hospitals will all be synchronized and prepared to act under the direction of our American Civil Defense force in time of emergency. Our American Civil Defense will coordinate all of our internal security and preparedness requirements. It will make sure we are ready to confront any threat on our homeland.

Our American Civil Defense force must secure the gaps in our homeland security. Our airports must be free from all potential threats from hijacking and terrorism. All luggage and cargo on our commercial passenger flights must be checked—without exception. We must have federal air marshals on every domestic and foreign flight—without exception. We must search every ocean-going vessel that attempts to enter an American seaport—without exception. We must demand that our power plants, our infrastructure and our natural resources are protected and defended from those that would seek to bring harm to America.

Our American Civil Defense force will defend our homeland by not permitting our borders to be so porous so as to allow foreign nationals to cross into our country at some remote location. We must have security across our expansive borders with Canada to the North and Mexico to the South. We must utilize our advantage in technology to make this a reality. Our Civil Defense force will use unmanned aerial surveillance and manned vehicle patrols to be confident that our borders are secure.

As Americans, we must be prepared for any eventuality. We must demand that our federal government do everything it can to prepare for any attacks against America. A unified American Civil Defense will solve security problems and allow us to have a proactive and flexible force that will secure our American homeland.

The American Civil Defense program will require new federal funding for fire, police and emergency medical technicians that are based in our population centers. We cannot allow political or special interest demands to restrict our preparedness. We must be confident in our reaction abilities to threats and attacks on our American homeland. Our hospital facilities must be ready for any medical need. Our fire, police and emergency medical technicians—our first-responders—must have the tools they need to take on any eventuality. We cannot allow ourselves to be short handed when it comes to the defense of our American homeland.

It is a common American necessity that our government put these safeguards into place immediately. I can think of no better place for our government to act in the American best interest. These security necessities are beyond partisanship, beyond regional interests—these are American requirements. We can create a safer country for ourselves and our children if we demand that our government do its job and protect the citizenry and homeland. We must be confident that our nation is prepared for any eventuality. A unified and proactive American Civil Defense force will achieve this goal.

Automobile Renewable Resources Commitment

America cannot ensure a secure homeland and a prosperous economic future if we remain dependent upon finite natural resources. We must make the change now to renewable resources powered by American technology.

As Americans, we must confront the fact that we are increasingly reliant on foreign nations to sell us the oil and gasoline for our automobiles. This is a reality we can no longer deny. They charge us outrageous prices because they know we are dependent. If oil-producing nations such as Saudi Arabia were to stop selling fuel to America or continue to raise their already exorbitant prices, our nation will grind to a stop—causing more economic damage than we can imagine. Our national security and our economic prosperity are at risk. We cannot continue to be dependent on finite resources and the good will of other nations to power our economy.

If we are going to build a common American future, one where we can ensure all of the freedoms and opportunities we have grown so accustomed to, then we simply must act to end our dependence on nonrenewable resources. Our love of cars and trucks and the freedom to travel is at the root of this issue. It's as simple as this: as Americans, we can drive whatever, wherever and whenever we want to and we can guarantee the same for our children, if we demand the investment into and utilization of renewable resource technology.

If we fail to act, not only will our national security and our economic opportunities be at risk, we cannot guarantee that the natural beauty—the air and the water of this great country—can be maintained for future generations to enjoy. We simply must act now to build a future for our children and stop living as though tomorrow does not matter. Creating, investing, researching, producing and distributing renewable resources will only serve to grow our security, create new jobs and make our lives and our environment healthier.

American Ethos is about recognizing the ideals we have in common, such as protecting our national security, securing our economic future, ensuring the freedom to travel for ourselves and our children and defending the environment. These are basic principles, ones all Americans consider important. We must translate these shared ideals into tangible action by making financial investments into renewable resources and adding federal mandates and tax incentives. When we unify, moving proactively as Americans with a common future interest, we can achieve that future. We can make renewable resource vehicles our reality.

I believe the federal government should use all of its resources to encourage the private development and investment into renewable resource technologies for automobiles immediately. I propose that the production of automobiles that only use non-renewable resources, specifically fossil fuels, be phased out over a 10 year period. The initial step towards this goal must be a legislative and financial commitment by the federal government—they must lead the way. The first year of this commitment would require a law passed by the federal government outlining milestones, responsibilities and funding, including taxes and incentives. Research grants and tax credits will be utilized to start the process and encourage private research and development. The next few years would see legislatively mandated steps, including the establishment of the best renewable resources for mass production and mass distribution, the development and investment into these renewable resources and the phasing in of requirements, such as an increasing number of vehicles being produced annually utilizing renewable resource fuel sources.

Over these 10 years, taxes will be levied against fossil fuel production and usage, the proceeds from which will be applied directly to the private research and development of renewable resources. Companies will receive tax credits for their commitment to research and development of renewable resource technology. Patents will be awarded to encourage competition and development. The goal is the development of a diverse and competitive fleet of renewable resources vehicles that will make our nation and our economy secure.

America is already on the way to a fossil fuel free automotive future. We already have hybrid vehicles that utilize electric power and have conventional fossil fuel back up engines. Let these vehicles be a first step in our evolution into a renewable resource future.

This commitment to renewable resources will require action on the part of all Americans. Each of us has a vested interest in our freedom from fossil fuels. Our federal government must utilize financial incentives to assist and encourage Americans as we make this change. To start, individuals will receive significant tax deductions for purchasing renewable resources vehicles. Additionally, I propose a trade-in solution whereby Americans with fossil fuel vehicles will be able to trade-in the value of their fossil fuel vehicle and receive a commensurate discount toward the purchase of a new renewable resource vehicle. Auto-dealers will be given tax credits for purchasing fossil fuel vehicles back as well as the opportunity to sell the used fossil fuel vehicles to foreign consumers. Only through a cooperative solution, all aspects of our nation working together, will we be able to move away from our dependence on fossil fuels.

The development of renewable resources for America will mean the creation of thousands of American jobs, diversification of American industries and long term American economic growth. American automotive companies already have the research and technology capacity to make renewable resources a reality for all Americans. But we as American consumers must demand renewable resources for all of our automobiles. We must demand that renewable resources be produced in amounts that compel manufacturers and retailers to produce and sell vehicles that use these renewable resources. We can create a supply by making a demand.

As Americans, it is our shared responsibility and our common security necessity that we move to renewable resources for our automobiles immediately.

100% American Defense Procurement

As Americans, we must demand that our military procurement be made in America, thereby growing our economy, creating jobs for Americans and assuring our military is self-sufficient. The outsourcing of our security is unacceptable.

I believe that we must demand that our American workforce, our technological and industrial base, must be the single provider and supplier to our American military. We simply cannot feel confident in our security if we are dependent on foreign governments and foreign companies to supply our military necessities.

Currently, 50% of American military procurement is required by law to be American made. I simply believe that this is insufficient to protect our American best interest. Our American military must serve the American citizenry, by not only defending us but also by becoming fully integrated into the American Ethos. When our military is 100% American made we will not only be more secure, we will bolster our economy through the creation of long term American jobs.

The most important responsibility of our American military is to defend the American homeland and its citizenry. For our military to be able to meet this responsibility, we must cultivate a competitive marketplace for American military industry and technology companies to grow and expand. We cannot count on just one American company to supply our military needs. We must build a diverse and viable defense industry of American companies. These American companies will hire, train and provide long term employment for American citizens and be prepared to supply the needs of the American military, not only permanently but also independent of foreign resources.

Removal of Weapons of Mass Destruction

America will not be made to live under the threat of weapons of mass destruction. We will use any and all available means to remove this threat.

The single most dangerous threat against America is the proliferation of weapons of mass destruction—chemical, biological and nuclear weapons. Whether in the hands of belligerent foreign states or terrorists, these threats will only continue to grow, bringing fear to our children and our way of life if we do not act immediately. It is our shared obligation and our common security necessity that weapons that could end our way of life be addressed.

We must demand that our federal government search unceasingly to find verifiable evidence of the propagation of weapons of mass destruction and that everything in our power as a nation be used to remove these threats. Once weapons that could cause harm to America are found, we must demand swift and effective action by our elected officials and our federal government to end the danger using any and all necessary means.

American Ethos means being progressive in the face of undeniable facts. Specific knowledge and evidence of weapons of mass destruction in the hands of belligerent foreign states or terrorist organizations is a reality we cannot accept. We simply must act as though our future depends on it, because it does. We must demand that progressive action be taken by our leader to protect our nation and our citizenry from the threat of weapons of mass destruction.

We must be willing to utilize diplomatic and economic means while we work with foreign nations to solve the threat that weapons of mass destruction present. We must work with the International Atomic Energy Commission and other international bodies to ensure that inspections and verifications are ongoing. We must employ and expand programs that allow us to purchase dangerous weapons and weapons materials from foreign countries, such as the Megatons for Megawatts program with Russia. In this program, old Soviet-era nuclear weapons are being purchased by America for use as civilian nuclear power fuel. I believe we must expand the Megatons for Megawatts program to all nuclear weaponized nations that are in any way threatening to our defense and security. We can create cheap and safe power for Americans and remove a security risk at the same time. If belligerent nations are unwilling to sell their nuclear weapons as fuel, all other means must be explored to remove these weapons as threats against America.

When all other means to end the threat of weapons of mass destruction have been explored, when peaceful means have been exhausted, military force may be necessary. When this becomes a reality, we cannot shy away. We must not wait to be attacked before we act. When we use military force to remove the threat of weapons of mass destruction, we should act to not only remove the threat permanently, we must also act to send a message to the world—America will not be threatened. We will not sit idly by while gathering threats grow around us. We will act to preserve and protect our citizenry and our way of life.

American Ethos demands that belligerent countries with weapons of mass destruction must confront a choice. They can remove their weapons through peaceful negotiation, verifiable reprocessing and destruction or they can meet with the full force of the American military that will have a singular responsibility, to remove the threat against America.

Global AIDS Treatment and Eradication

If unchecked, AIDS will continue to bring instability and death to the world. We have a common obligation and owe it to our children to rid the world of the blight of AIDS.

I believe it is imperative to the security of America that we treat and eradicate Acquired Immune Deficiency Syndrome (AIDS) around the world. Our future security, economic dominance and the health of each and everyone of us demands that we act decisively to combat AIDS around the world.

I believe we as Americans have a moral responsibility to fight against death and misery wherever it is found and AIDS continues to be a primary cause of death and misery around the world. This must be addressed immediately. It is our responsibility as we are the only nation capable of making the commitments necessary to defeat AIDS. When we do act, other capable countries must be encouraged to step in and provide assistance as well. We have the resources, both financial and pharmaceutical, and the relationships internationally, to beat AIDS. We must not let our religious, cultural, political or economic differences interfere with the treatment of AIDS as a national security threat. AIDS is a shared danger. We must act on all fronts—treating the infected, teaching the young and stabilizing regions and governments.

AIDS is a serious health threat to all Americans that must be confronted. However, the more immediate threat from the effects of AIDS is on governments and countries around the world. War, refugees, instability as well as financial and economic turmoil around the globe will ensue unless we act against AIDS on a mass scale. If we continue to fail to act decisively, AIDS will grow out of control, destabilizing governments and causing global insecurity. We must deal with AIDS now to prevent the effects of global instability leading to insecurity at home.

We as Americans must demand that our elected leaders put aside their ideological and political differences and commit to defeating AIDS. Our shared national security is at stake. We must begin by tapping our vast research and development base. Through the usage of tax incentives and patent rights, we must encourage our American pharmaceutical companies to create new and innovative answers to AIDS, including a vaccine for the uninfected and affordable long term treatment for the infected. We must work through international organizations, such as the United Nations, to address needs and distribute medical supplies. We must encourage the usage of any methods and tools that promote activities that reduce the transmission of AIDS, regardless of our individual moral beliefs.

I firmly believe that America must play a leading role in the peace and security of the world. Providing treatment, prevention and stability where AIDS festers is a significant step we can take to provide that peace and security to the world and more importantly, to America.

Foreign Financial Aid Reform

Our American resources must not be wasted overseas on propping up foreign governments when they can be better spent on strengthen our American homeland.

America is a country blessed with an abundance of wealth and ability. With our great affluence and power comes great responsibility. We must be an active participant in the cause of peace around the world. We must continue to work with the United Nations and international aid programs to combat poverty, hunger and homeless around the world. Programs such as the United States Agency for International Development must be fully funded. The USAID programs serve the civilian populations of foreign nations, allowing Americans to directly assist those in need by addressing necessities such as food, water, shelter and medicine. We must take our rightful place in the world community by providing necessities to the impoverished. If we do not provide these necessities, we will be creating breeding grounds of instability that will lead to insecurity in America. It is our moral obligation and our security requirement that we help foreign civilian populations rise out of poverty, while maintaining the defense of America as our first priority.

Providing necessities to foreign civilian populations does not mean we should sustain foreign governments because of political expediency. It is not our responsibility to spend our hard earned American dollars keeping a foreign government in place. The success or failure of regimes abroad that have clearly become dependent on American financial aid must not be our primary concern. If there is a revolution in a foreign country because a government cannot stand without American financial aid, then America must be on the side of the people, the foreign citizenry, not one government or dominate power. It is not our place to disrupt the political evolution of foreign nations.

Every year, our federal government gives tens of billions of dollars directly to foreign countries to stabilize their governments. This must end. If a foreign government cannot stand on its own, through the support of its own population, American taxpayer funds should not be used to bolster these regimes. Foreign aid to governments does not bring long term security to America; it instead leads to anger and resentment against America. I simply believe that these tens of billions of dollars in annual foreign aid funds could be better utilized in America, for American security at home.

For America to be secure in the future, we must be viewed as an honest broker in the world. We have both a moral obligation and a security requirement to be an active and positive force in the world. We must allow the natural development of foreign nations, stand for basic human rights and better the plight of foreign civilians that are in need. But, we must not falsely empower foreign governments, subverting natural political evolution with American dollars better spent at home.

Legalization for Qualified Undocumented Workers

Our national immigration policy toward the millions of undocumented workers and illegal immigrants who live and work in America is untenable and overdue for the reforms of the America Ethos.

I believe that our defense and economy can only grow and prosper if we bring rationality into our immigration policy. The fact is, our service sector and our farming industry depend on the labor that undocumented workers already provide. They are essential to our economy and our security. We must act to recognize this reality with a program of incremental legalization that will increase our homeland defense, bolster our economy and expand our tax base.

Today, millions of undocumented workers are already working and living in America, providing essential labor to our economy and by law, receiving social services. Should they not be legalized and recognized and pay taxes, becoming part of the American community? I believe they should. Is it more feasible to offer a regulated process of legalization that identifies and investigates immigrants, or round up the millions of undocumented workers that our economy depends on and deport them? I believe that legalization is the only solution that meets our economic and security needs.

It is unacceptable and immoral that we have an underclass of illegal and undocumented workers living in America, and yet, they are essential to American prosperity. A legalization program that brings these people into the system, vetting them, allowing Americans to know who is here and what their intentions are, will not only serve to bolster our economy, increase our security and grow our American Ethos, it is also the right thing to do.

As Americans, we must face the fact that having millions of undocumented workers and illegal immigrants living and working in America is a security risk we cannot continue to blindly accept. These undocumented workers and illegal immigrants are legally receiving social welfare, such as education at public schools and Medicare. However, employers, knowing that their employment is illegal, rarely if ever deduct taxes. Our economy is dependent on these undocumented workers and yet we have no way of knowing who they are or if they represent a security threat. These disconnects cannot stand. We must bring the rationality and progressiveness of the American Ethos into our immigration policy.

I propose an incremental program whereby illegal immigrants and undocumented workers can gain legalized status in America. This legalization program will begin with applications for permanent residency, in-depth and comprehensive background checks, fingerprinting and personal interviews. Criminals and threats to America must be detained and deported immediately. Only illegal immigrants and undocumented workers who are in America and are employed will be permitted to apply for legalization. Employers of the undocumented workers will be offered amnesty from prosecution from broken immigration and employment laws if they are willing to sponsor their undocumented and illegal employees. If the employers are unwilling to participate, the full force of our immigration and employment laws will be used to demand compliance. The undocumented workers will be offered permanent residency regardless of their illegal entry into America. If they wish to stay, be vetted and become part of the system, we will welcome them. They will work, be taxed and become fully integrated into our American Ethos.

This incremental legalization proposal will require cooperation from all parties involved. Employers must be willing to work with their illegal employees to find an equitable solution. Undocumented workers and illegal immigrants must be willing to step forward and be vetted for their eligibility to become legalized. Our government through our American Civil Defense force will ensure that our borders cease to be revolving doors to illegal immigrants. Only through a legalization procedure will we be able to determine who is a security risk and who is simply an immigrant, searching for a better life. Only through cooperation can any of this occur.

Our country was founded by the immigration of peoples from around the world who were searching and hoping for a better life. Our history is marked by the immigration of peoples from South America, Europe, Asia and Africa, all of whom came here under unique situations—some legally, some illegally, some willingly, some unwillingly. Immigrants came to America as slaves, religious, economic or political refugees. Each group of people that came to America has added to the greater whole, regardless of the how and why they came, creating the great American melting pot that makes us unique in the world. Immigration to America has never been easy. Immigrants have had to contend with racism and intolerance in this country, but they have persevered to earn an equal and rightful place in America. Immigration is as American as our Constitution. It is simply an essential component of our history. We must recognize that our nation is truly blessed to have such as diverse population. This immigrant diversity is our strength.

Immigration is an American issue, one we must deal with openly, fairly and without the intrusion of unnecessary partisanship or social value judgments. Our economic prosperity and our national security demand progressive action. It is time we utilize our immigrant strength and move forward as a unified nation with a regulated plan to legalize our undocumented workers and increase our economic and national security.

Federal regulations on voting standards and procedures

As American owner-operators of this representative democracy, we must demand federally mandated voting procedures that are trustworthy, unbiased and consistent state by state.

I believe that it is the responsibility of our federal government to ensure that all federal elections are conducted in such a manner as to assure that results are not only timely and accurate but are overtly open, fair and consistent state by state. As Americans, we must demand that our Constitutional obligation to vote is precise and reliable. Anything less and we will not build faith into our electoral process and our representative government. I believe we must utilize the best American-made technology available to create a consistent voting standard for all Americans.

The federal government must mandate and fund voting standards and procedures for all states and localities to adhere to. New voting machines, using the most advanced and reliable technologies, must be utilized. We must demand safeguards, such as paper receipts and redundancies, to ensure accuracy. We must utilize all technological means to verify identity and create easily accessible and easily understood standardized voting procedures that guarantee exact and fast results. We must be aware of and defend against any efforts to manipulate or coerce our voting procedures that would allow partisanship and special interests to distort or otherwise influence our electoral process.

As Americans, we all share a common obligation to make certain that our democracy is just and reliable. Regardless of our partisan affiliation, we all have an interest in a free and fair election system. If we are going to build an American Ethos and restore our trust and faith in American democracy, we simply cannot stand for permitting our most sacred Constitutional obligation to be manipulated by inaccuracy and fraud. We cannot allow special interests and partisanship to continue to permit legal loopholes and unreliable voting procedures to continue.

Federal voting standards that mandate consistency, openness, accuracy and accountability must be demanded by the American people and enacted by the federal government immediately.

Federal Election Holiday

A federal holiday on the day we vote for our federal representatives will serve to elevate this democratic responsibility to the place it deserves.

I believe that the first Tuesday in November of every other year should be a federal holiday. Citizens should be given this day to contemplate and fulfill their Constitutional obligation to vote.

It is a terrible injustice that our shared Constitutional obligation to vote is being ignored by over half of our population. I believe we must set aside a day where the normal responsibilities of work are set aside so that we can reinforce our rights by thoughtfully electing representatives. We can honor this Constitutional obligation and enfranchise countless Americans by instituting an election holiday.

◆   ◆   ◆

The Perpetual Creation of Jobs

The creation of good paying, secure jobs with healthcare benefits and opportunities for advancement—jobs that allow Americans to work for each other, doing something of value for the community—this should be the priority of the federal government. This is the goal of the American Ethos.

American Ethos is based on the idea of creating national unity through progressive action. A job for every American is an indispensable element to this unity. I believe it is simply essential to our future as a people and as a nation that we focus our collective efforts on creating jobs for all Americans. I believe it is the responsibility of our federal government to create and cultivate an economic environment where American jobs are being created in every sector of our economy.

American Ethos is cultivated when all Americans know they are part of the national fabric, one in which they are contributing to the greater good. Our future has more meaning and purpose; we have more control over our lives when we have access to secure jobs. When we have jobs and are contributing to society, we care more for our neighbors and countrymen. When we are invested into our country through our community and our job, we are contributing to the American Ethos. The creation of jobs at all levels, utilizing all skill sets and all industries, will grow our economy and expand our American Ethos.

As America moves into the global economy, it must lead. No American wants to see our world-leading standard of living diminished. We want our children to be able to have the same opportunities or better. If we are going to make this a reality, then we must prepare for the challenges that free trade and global competition present.

We must fight the outsourcing of skilled positions to foreign nations with cheap labor and the mass industrial and manufacturing migrations to many of the same foreign countries. If we do not act, we will lose our economic superiority. We must cultivate an American technological, industrial and commercial base that creates jobs and economic prosperity for Americans.

It is the responsibility of every American and moreover, the primary responsibility of our elected federal government, to ensure that the American economy is setting the standard in the global market place, and thereby ensuring the perpetual creation of American jobs. When the federal government can create an environment for job creation, using all available means, spreading the growth across the entire economy, touching every industry and every community, there is a commensurate expansion in national spirit. American Ethos means the creation of good paying, secure jobs with healthcare benefits and opportunities for advancement for all Americans.

Infrastructure Reinvestment

Our American Ethos depends on our shared commitment to each other and our future. Building a common future requires investment into our shared assets as a nation. We must invest into America and create jobs for Americans by investing into the infrastructure of America.

Cultivating an American Ethos means learning to work together, building partnerships between all levels of government as well as private business to grow our economy and to create American jobs. Investing into our common resources—our shared infrastructure—provides an excellent opportunity to create American jobs, better our nation and grow our national spirit. An Infrastructure Reinvestment Program led by the federal government which will work with states, municipalities and private business, to facilitate and fund infrastructure projects in urban and rural areas across America, will grow our national spirit and create American jobs.

As Americans, we must confront the fact that the infrastructure of America is dilapidated and in need of immediate reinvestment and rebuilding. Across America, schools and hospitals, roads and bridges, dams and sewers, electrical grids and mass transportation systems are in desperate straits and need to be rebuilt and reinvested into immediately.

The last time a massive infrastructure reinvestment program was initiated in America was during the great depression of the 1930's. The New Deal of President Franklin Roosevelt led to the creation of millions of jobs at a time when the economy was not able to create sufficient jobs for American needs. Americans across this land took up jobs and created most of the factories, roads, tunnels and bridges we have today. It is now time, some 70 years later, to reinvest into the infrastructure of our great nation.

The goal of the Infrastructure Reinvestment Program is to unify state and local government proposals, work with state and local businesses, utilizing state and local resources and create state and local jobs. These infrastructure projects will range from rebuilding schools and hospitals to improving water quality within a municipality by rebuilding sewage and piping, building water treatment plants and irrigating an area for farming. We will invest into our transportation system by repairing and building bridges and tunnels, expanding roads and highways to ease traffic or building a rail system between cities. Our electrical system, our seaports, our airports, our towns and cities all have infrastructure needs that must be met and will simultaneously create jobs and grow our American Ethos.

The federal government will receive proposals from states and municipalities for infrastructure rebuilding projects at the local level. It will be up to the states and municipalities to decide where best to invest in their communities. The federal government will ensure that the projects are in line with anticorruption laws, federal civil rights laws and safe construction practice. Otherwise, I believe that the federal government should be the funds provider, underwriter, initiator and facilitator helping to create jobs and investment at the local level, not overburdening with pointless federal regulations that would only serve to slow and confuse the process.

Federal, state and local governments must work together to finance infrastructure reinvestment projects. We must set priorities at the state and local level while the federal government can then take a leadership role in funding and facilitating compromise. The federal government can set out a grant toward the projects which would be matched by state, municipal and private contributions. If loans are needed, the federal government should underwrite the terms and guarantee the loan. Progressive growth and unity can only be achieved when we recognize that shared responsibility and mutual benefit are essential to our American future.

These local infrastructure improvements would help Americans in their quality of life everyday. Americans will live in and around these tangible improvements. These infrastructure projects would employ local people in construction and trades, such as electrical and plumbing, and then teachers and nurses as well as expanding the local tax base.

Growing our economy is our shared responsibility. If we are willing to invest into our infrastructure and thereby our future, we can create good paying, secure jobs for our fellow Americans, while expanding our economy and building a common American spirit through mutually beneficial achievement to be shared by all Americans.

Job Creation through Tax Incentives

American Ethos demands progressive partnerships between American businesses and the American government to get Americans back to work. If we can cultivate the economic conditions whereby American jobs are created, we are growing our national unity and developing our shared economic strength. I believe that it is in our common best interest that we spur American job growth through targeted tax breaks for American businesses.

During the economic boom of the 1990's our economy grew and our national debt diminished for one simply reason, more tax paying American citizens were employed. Our economic expansion was not because of an overvalued stock market or unnecessary tax increases. It was American companies that were able to hire, train and employ Americans across all skill levels. I believe that it is our shared obligation as Americans to again create these economic conditions and cultivate American job growth, across all industries and all skill levels.

Our federal government and its tax structure must not act as an impediment to the creation of American jobs through American businesses. I believe that it is the obligation of our federal government to build the economic conditions and cultivate relationships with American businesses whereby American jobs are created.

I propose a program where public and private corporations and businesses doing business in America are offered substantial tax breaks if they meet two conditions: while doing business in America, they must hire only American citizens or permanent residents and they must provide some level of health insurance for their employees. If these two basic requirements can be met by American businesses, then I believe we as a people through our federal government will have achieved our American Ethos goal of cultivating an economic environment whereby good paying, secure American jobs with healthcare benefits and opportunities for advancement jobs are being created.

National Service Consolidation—American Community Corps

Compulsory national service will better prepare our children for their future by giving them valuable employment experience, maturity and the recognition that they are part of the American Ethos through a shared experience in building a better future.

Cultivating an American Ethos requires the recognition that being an American demands sacrifices and commitments. Our American freedoms must be earned everyday by defending our country, our Constitution and collectively building an America that is prepared for the future. It is essential to the future growth of our nation that we cultivate our common American experience while building a trained workforce that is prepared to compete in the global market place. American Ethos means investing into our freedom, ourselves and our future.

As Americans, we must understand that we are more than individuals fighting for our own interests. We are all Americans—striving for a better future for ourselves, our neighbors and our children. We must build our common future with mutually beneficial actions today. We must cultivate common ties between us as Americans—ties that bind us together in mutually beneficial shared experiences.

I believe that the best way to build a trained workforce and cultivate an American bond is to consolidate our national service programs and make national service compulsory for every American. I propose the consolidation of the four major service programs, AmeriCorps, Take Pride in America, City Year and USA Freedom Corps, under one new program: the American Community Corps.

The American Community Corps would require the compulsory service of every American, beginning at the age of 18, lasting for 12 months. This service to the country would include military, civil defense, local civilian safety such as fire, police and emergency medical services and providing manpower for needed areas, such as urban and rural teaching assistants, medical staff and especially infrastructure reinvestment projects.

The American Community Corps would meet the immediate needs of the country by asking the service of young Americans ready to better their country and invest into their future. I envision an American Community Corps worker that has a choice where they serve and how they serve. A Community Corps worker living in Oklahoma could choose to serve as a trainee in a local fire or police department. A Community Corps worker in New York could serve by working on infrastructure reinvestment projects. A Community Corps worker from California could serve as a trainee teacher to school districts in need. Through partnerships with state and local governments and businesses, Community Corps workers would be assigned to a team and a project. They would be provided training, tools and a task. Community Corps workers would be given a small salary and subsidized housing. Utilizing federal, state and local grants, as well as tax-deductible business contributions, we can fund the Community Corps.

I believe in a Community Corps that is compulsory for everyone, regardless of race, religion, gender, disability or economic status. How Americans serve is not as important as the service itself. In whatever capacity Americans serve, the shared experience will be uniquely American and will serve to build our national unity while training the future American workforce.

The goal is to provide American Community Corps workers with valuable skills for their future while investing into their country. After Community Corps workers complete their service, they will be more qualified to enter the workforce and recruited by employers, college and universities. I believe that a well-trained, unified workforce of Americans is the best way we can maintain our economic dominance in the world. A compulsory national service program will create such a workforce.

Outsourcing Moratorium

We must keep highly skilled technology, manufacturing and industrial jobs based in America—especially when our unemployment rate is at unacceptable levels.

As we move into the new millennium and meet the challenges of the global economy, we must be prepared to defend American jobs. We simply cannot tolerate the export of American jobs to foreign nations that offer little more than cheap labor. It is our shared responsibility as Americans to defend our workforce and protect our American way of life.

We must confront the fact that the outsourcing of skilled positions in industries such as technology and manufacturing is a reality in the global economy. Our competitors in the new millennium, China and India, offer skilled labor at a fraction of the cost as in America, simply because they have not reached our unique standard of living. As Americans, we have a shared obligation to meet this challenge. We must protect our economic dominance and ensure our standard of living for future generations.

We must demand that American companies make every effort to utilize American workers to fill skilled positions in every industry. If education or retraining is required, our government and our businesses must invest into the American worker. Our American workforce must be the first priority.

Many Americans have already lost their jobs to outsourcing and continue to have difficulty finding new jobs. This trend will only continue if we do not act immediately. We cannot sit passively as American businesses send American jobs overseas at a time when Americans who are ready, willing and able to work, but are turned away in place of cheaper foreign labor.

I propose a moratorium on the outsourcing of highly skilled positions to foreign counties when the unemployment rate in America reaches a certain level. If American companies continue to outsource American jobs in the face of this unemployment based moratorium, these American companies will be fined by the federal government. These fines will be directed exclusively to the retraining of American workers and specifically to those directly affected by the outsourcing. The goal is to take the incentive out of outsourcing and to create American jobs and American prosperity.

In the global economy of the new millennium, American business is either with the American people or against the American people. American Ethos demands that American businesses and private enterprise, the originator of the American prosperity we have grown to love, must defend the American workforce and stop giving our unequaled standard of living away to foreign nations with cheap labor.

Trade Expansion and Intellectual Property Protection

Our American economy has grown and prospered because of capitalism, fair international trade and the opening of markets. Now is the time to expand our economy and create job opportunities for Americans through the expansion of fair international trade.

Where we can grow our economy and create better, more productive employment for Americans through international trade, we must act. We must demand open foreign markets and fair trading relationships that will allow our economy to thrive. Building mutually beneficial relationships with foreign nations based on trade will ensure long term American job growth and economic prosperity.

To ensure our economic security, we must cultivate broad trading relationships with developing nations. The countries of China and India represent about half of the world's population. They are in the early stages of becoming industrial, commercial and technological superpowers. Their untapped markets represent long term growth for our economy and employment for Americans for generations to come. We must utilize our dominance in productivity and technology to take advantage of their ongoing development and become long term trading partners.

We must establish trading relationships that create jobs for Americans and benefit our industrial, commercial and manufacturing sectors through the production and export of American made goods and services. We must ensure that our American intellectual property is protected from piracy. We must not sacrifice American jobs to build up foreign nations. Above all, fair trade must be fair to the American worker.

American Ethos believes in the American economy, American businesses and the American worker. We can compete with any nation in the world based on our dominating productivity and technology. We work harder and smarter than anyone. Our American ingenuity and business enterprise are essential to the future success of our economy. Our ability to invest, manufacture, mass produce and distribute goods and services is unmatched in the world. This must be reinforced. It is our shared responsibility as Americans to protect our creativity and our world leading productivity by fighting against the corrosive forces of piracy and trademark infringement.

We must act to protect our nation's ability to invent new and creative solutions to the issues and problems of our world. We must protect the ability of American companies and entrepreneurs to not only create, but also to ensure long term returns on these creations. We must defend our American companies as they compete in the global marketplace through federal government enforcement of intellectual property laws in all trading relationships.

I believe that any product made or designed in America must have permanent intellectual property, trademark and copyright ownership based in America. Every time that product is sold, it must benefit American companies financially, no matter where it was produced, thereby growing the American economy and creating American jobs.

As Americans we have a shared interest in fighting against unfair trade. When a foreign nation violates anti-piracy laws, ignores American intellectual property laws—when foreign nations will not permit American products to be sold in their country or apply tariffs, a commensurate fine, ban or tariff must be imposed.

American Ethos demands our federal government defend our economic future. Expanding fair trade is vital to our shared economic future. Our nation must never become dependent on trade with foreign nations, nor should we allow our ethnic, religious or political differences to restrict our opportunities to grow our economy. The goal is to grow the American economy and create American jobs. Global trade that is fair to the American worker is an opportunity that we must pursue, cultivate and dominate.

Research and Development Initiative

America must be the definitive leader in the research and development of new and revolutionary technology in the new millennium. We must make a commitment as a nation to build a research and development base that encourages innovation, business growth and long term American job creation.

Every economic boom in America has at its roots revolutionary technological advancement. Through American innovation, research and dedication, our nation has walked on the moon, cured diseases and developed the internet. These leaps in technology have created new and vibrant industries and jobs for Americans. It is our shared obligation to once again create and cultivate a research and development base in America that will grow our national unity and create jobs for Americans.

I propose a research and development initiative led by the federal government, in cooperation with public and private enterprise, to encourage the development of new technologies, products and services that will not only grow the economy and create American jobs, but will help Americans in everyday life. America must find the cures to diseases, more efficient energy sources and better methods of communication. America must lead the world scientific research and development.

The federal government should utilize tax breaks for businesses that engage in new and innovative research and development as well as grants and loans to those brave Americans willing to take the risks necessary to find new technology and create new American jobs. We must utilize copyright, trademark and anti-piracy laws to cultivate growth. We must encourage new exploration in biomedical and genetic research, renewable resources, agricultural innovation and expanding the internet and information technology. These new industries will be the foundation for the American economy and job creation in the future.

Where American ingenuity and creativity can build a better way, our federal government must encourage it using any and all available means. American economic growth and the expansion of a highly developed, competitive and productive America workforce are crucial to our future.

Our children deserve the same opportunities we have and more, but this will not happen on its own. We must unify and ensure that America leads the world in the research and development of new and innovative products and services and thereby create long term jobs for Americans for generations to come.

◆   ◆   ◆

Universal Standards in Education

American Ethos affirms that education—equal, efficient and locally controlled education—is essential to our democracy. As Americans, we have a shared responsibility to ensure that our education system is second to none in the world.

For America to be dominant in the future, we must invest into the education of our children. They must be given the skills to take advantage of the economic opportunities and challenges of the future. We must build an adaptive and prepared workforce that will create and fill the jobs that the global economy demands. I believe it is the responsibility of our federal government to ensure our American education system is fully supported, fully funded and operating at the highest possible level.

We must recognize that the current state of our education system requires the attention of all Americans. When too many school districts have dangerous buildings, overburdened teachers and insufficient technology for students, we must collectively move to remedy the problem. Many American communities are confronted with school districts that are severely under funded and being supported only by the devotion of parents, staff and administrators at the local level that are the last line of defense. This cannot stand. As Americans, we must act with a unified spirit to guarantee that our education system breeds success and is given the resources and direction to give America a future of unity and economic prosperity.

American Ethos is the recognition that the federal government cannot and should not dictate to states and localities how we educate our children. However, the federal government and our elected representatives must play an essential role in ensuring equitable funding and setting basic standards that all American schools must strive to attain.

As Americans, we all have a vested interest in seeing that our education system and all of our schools meet high standards. Urban or rural, large or small—all schools must be challenged to breed excellence. I believe that the answers are on the local level. I believe in public school education and the professional teacher. Public school teachers with the right tools, skills and experience make positive lifelong impacts on students' lives that must be encouraged. We must recognize that it is the responsibility of all Americans to play a vital role in the education of our children.

Cultivating an American Ethos means recognizing our public schools for the important place they hold in our society. Only at our local public schools can all Americans, regardless of their race, religion or culture, meet to find common ground. It is on this common ground that we find our American Ethos. We must invest and develop our education system with proactive measures from which all Americans can benefit. When we make a commitment to better the education of our children and building a diverse and adaptive workforce, we are guaranteeing our future cultivating an American Ethos.

New Schools Program

Investing into our public schools, making them the tools of our future economic prosperity, should be the crowning achievement in our building a common American spirit.

As part of the infrastructure reinvestment program, utilizing our American Community Corps and state and local businesses, I believe we should invest into our future by rebuilding old and building new public schools in every school district in need. I believe our public schools are the most important place in our community as there is no other place in our society where we can affect such an important and lasting change on our future. Our public schools should reflect our community and our shared commitment to our common future. Our public schools cannot be allowed to be dilapidated or useless. They must become more useful, more a part of our communities.

I believe there should be no reason that a child is unprepared to enter the adult world and workforce. We must remove the impediments of insufficient room space, dilapidated buildings and insufficient technology. We must cultivate an environment where students have the best opportunity to learn. We must guarantee that our public schools are secure, safe from weapons and disrepair and attentive to the needs of our children. They must feel safe in their school for learning to be effective.

Investing into our public schools is a long term investment into ourselves and the quality of life we enjoy while ensuring the same for our children. I believe we can do something positive, for the benefit of all Americans, by acting to improve public schools in need across America. The federal government should act with state and local government to identify problem areas in school districts. Where there is overcrowding, insufficient technology or decaying structures, we must act together—local, state and federal governments—to find remedies and make progress.

By investing into our schools, we can create jobs, empower our children and create a more secure future for all Americans. If we care about the next generation of Americans and if we want to guarantee our level of affluence, we simply must invest into our public schools.

National Education Standards and Testing

As Americans, it is in our common best interest to ensure that all Americans are entering adulthood and the global marketplace with a base level of knowledge. We owe it to our children and our fellow countrymen and women to set a standard for basic knowledge and an ever increasing level of education achievement.

America must ensure that its education system is serving its purpose and producing qualified, prepared and able young adults. We must make sure that graduates from our school systems hold basic skills in mathematics, literacy and civic responsibilities. We must establish federally mandated basic standards for our high school graduates to achieve prior to their matriculation into the adult workforce. These skills must be universally understood by Americans of this new millennium. Anything less will not serve our goal of cultivating a common American Ethos.

I propose a federally mandated and locally administered test that all graduating high school students must take and pass. The federal government should work with parents, teachers, administrators and employers to establish this basic skills test that will help every high school graduate to prosper in the future. If a student does not pass the test, they cannot be given the honor of a high school diploma. Those that have not obtained the universal skills in this test must receive continuing education, while they serve in the American Community Corps, until they achieve the proficiency necessary to pass this test.

I do not believe that these tests should be overly complicated. I envision a test with 3 sections; basic reading comprehension, such as reading and understanding a newspaper story, basic mathematics, such as addition, subtraction, multiplication and division, and basic life skills, such as civic responsibilities and budgeting. I envision a test for students that is the culmination of their high school and life experiences—one that allows the rest of America to know that, at the very least, high school graduates will enter the world with basic, commonly-held skills.

The TVCC Program

Our technical, vocational and community colleges are essential to the development and retraining of our American workforce, especially when they have been displaced by global competition.

The TVCC program has as its purpose the investment of resources into our technical, vocational and community colleges. These schools are perpetually under funded and under utilized, yet they are often the best place to help fellow Americans retrain after changing careers and to give young Americans a chance to educate themselves beyond the high school level. I believe we should invest into our local TVCCs to better our fellow Americans and to guarantee our future economic superiority.

Our TVCCs must have the resources necessary to assist our fellow Americans as they help themselves. I believe that it is the responsibility of our federal government to provide the resources and direction necessary to give our TVCCs the ability to retrain the American worker and grow the American economy.

I propose that the federal government create a program whereby the local TVCCs apply for grants and low cost loans directly from the federal government. These grants and loans should be geared toward bringing new technology and modernization at TVCCs: new buildings, new instructors, new programs and creating scholarships for students. If a student cannot afford to attend a TVCC, then the TVCC and the federal government should provide the tuition for the student, especially those students who have lost their jobs as a result of global competition and are taking the initiative to retrain themselves.

I believe the federal government can serve no greater purpose than to help fellow Americans who are investing into themselves. By investing into TVCCs we can help to assist fellow Americans to reenter the workforce with new and reinforced skills that benefit all Americans and grow the American economy.

Science and Technology Education Program

As Americans, we must cultivate a learning environment by insisting on a standard of technology in every public school across America. Technology, including computers and internet access for every school and every student must be guaranteed by the federal government, working in partnership with local and state government as well as private businesses.

We must prepare our children for the job opportunities of the future. We must encourage future software engineers, astronauts and biomedical researchers to complete their education. We must support our local public high schools as they educate our future scientists and technologists. Our federal government must set high standards, insisting on proper funding and competent instructors at the high school level. As Americans, it is our common responsibility to ensure that our children are educated and skilled in science and technology fields as these will guarantee our future economic prosperity.

I propose a program where high school students are given every opportunity, through commitments from government, businesses and universities, to develop their skills in science and technology fields. If a student is willing to take on the rigor of study needed to be successful in the fields of science and technology, then I believe that it is the responsibility of all Americans to support their education.

I believe that mentoring is an essential part of education, especially in science and technology fields. Utilizing tax credits, we must encourage current professionals in science and technology fields to contribute their time by instructing and motivating our students to continue their education. Hands-on participation by fellow Americans with knowledge and experience—sharing their expertise and assisting in the education of our children—is crucial to the advancement of our economy and the development of a skilled workforce.

We must encourage technology sharing, internships and apprentice programs that allow students to experience the real world. The federal government must work with research universities and private businesses to provide top of the line research tools including microscopes, telescopes, computers and information technology to our high schools. Those private businesses and science and technology professionals that are willing to participate in this program will be recognized with tax incentives.

When we cultivate a science and technology base in our country, one that provides skills and experience for our children to be able to dominate the global economy, we are acting with a common spirit and building our American Ethos.

Continuing Education for Instructors

Our American teachers are the most important tool we have to ensure our future as a free and prosperous America. We must ensure that they have the skills and assets needed to achieve our common goals.

We live in a complicated and changing world. New technologies and innovations are being discovered everyday. It is imperative that our teachers are able to keep up with this changing world. They must be encouraged to further their education. I believe that it is essential that our teachers are continually learning new theories and new methods of relaying information to students. This exchange of information between teacher and student is critical to the future of our nation. We must guarantee that the most updated and useful information is available to our students by insisting that our teachers continue their own education.

I propose a federal tax credit for educators that continue their education and further their teaching abilities. I believe that it is the responsibility of our federal government to act progressively to encourage this continuing education. We must establish a base level of continuing education requirements through working with teacher unions, school districts and state and local government. These requirements will be mandated by the federal government and left to states, localities and school districts to enforce. If state and local governments do not enforce federal continuing education mandates, they will be subject to federal sanctions, including fines. The continuing education of our teachers and the development of our students and children is the responsibility of all Americans.

I believe in the professional teacher and the essential role teachers play in the education of our children. Our teachers are vital to our future economic superiority. We must act to ensure that they have the skills necessary to help our children succeed and dominate in the global marketplace. Federally mandating continuing education for our educators achieves this goal.

◆   ◆   ◆

The American Ethos Presidency

The President of the United States should be the unbiased, definitive word on the American best interest. We deserve a President that is independent, not tied to liberal or conservative ideologies, not obligated to deep pocketed special interests—one that is committed to a single group, the American citizenry.

American Ethos is the idea that it is the duty of all Americans to take responsibility for our country and our representative government. We are all equally vested into our nation and share an obligation to become active owner-operators of our democracy—to demand action and lead by example. We must act by injecting the American Ethos ideals of unity and progressiveness into the power structure of our government. We must elect an American Ethos Presidency, one not tied to special interests or political party. We must elect a President that has one goal—to create and cultivate an American Ethos; building unity in America.

It is our shared responsibility as owner-operators of America to act now to limit the corrupting influences of partisanship and special interests on our democratic system of government. I believe that electing an American Ethos President that owes no allegiance or financial obligation to partisan or special interests—someone who can achieve unity and progress in the name of American idealism—will serve to counter the corrosive forces and restore our trust in representative government. An American Ethos Presidency that will champion our common goals and make us proud to be Americans will help us regain our ownership of America.

Over the past 50 years we, the American citizenry, have grown distrustful of our government. We have watched as partisan extremists and wealthy special interests dominate our government. Most Americans have grown so disgusted with the American political system, we don't contribute at all. We vote less, we participate less and we care less for our shared American future. We have become members of smaller and smaller interest groups that share increasingly little in common. We have allowed ourselves to be manipulated by groups that purport to represent our best interests. We are lured by our regionalism and our reactionism. Our cultural identification and our ideological beliefs pull us away from our common American idealism. This cannot stand. For America to endure in the next millennium, we simply must begin to view ourselves as Americans first—not a collection of competing minorities. Electing an American Ethos Presidency will bring us together around our commonly held beliefs and priorities.

We do not need to be dragged left and right by competing deep-pocketed special interests that, in the end, achieve nothing for the majority of Americans. I say: Let the special interests and political parties have their way with legislators in Congress, but the President should be above these partisan interest group battles. Let the President be the person that is the judge of what is best for all Americans, not the biased and conflicted interests of the powerful and influential few. Let an American Ethos President be a pragmatic and loyal servant of the American people.

I do not believe that special interests and partisanship should be shut out of government. I simply believe the Congress is the place for these concerns to be heard. The Congress allows representatives to aggressively represent their specific ideology and local interests. However, the Presidency must be above these ideological conflicts. Let the battles be fought in the Congress and then let an American Ethos Presidency decide what aspects of these partisan, special interest clashes is best for all Americans. If the Congress is to be overrun by extreme partisanship and special interests, then we must have one person, one office that is a last line of defense for the American best interest—an American Ethos President.

> An American Ethos President will limit the impact of partisanship and special interests by being an outsider to the system, someone who has not been tainted by the corrupting influences of partisanship and special interest money. Utilizing the American ideologies of transparent decision-making, fairness and progressiveness, an American Ethos President will liberate our federal government from corruption and will guarantee a political process that grows our America Ethos through the achievement of mutually beneficial goals.

> An American Ethos Presidency would serve as the Presidency was originally intended: an independent branch of government, acting as a check and balance against the legislature and the judiciary, representing and defending the American citizenry and the Constitution.

> An American Ethos Presidency would bring all sides together by pursuing policies and legislation that benefit all Americans. By taking the best points of each ideological argument and limiting special interest and partisan demands, an American Ethos President can help cultivate true bipartisan legislation that benefits the many.

> An American Ethos Presidency would demand a balance of ideas and perspectives: fighting against extremism and finding the best compromise, actually getting things done, making tangible progress towards goals that benefit all Americans.

> An American Ethos Presidency would represent all Americans and serve no particular religious or cultural interest but instead serve the greater good in the universal and inclusive concepts of kindness, charity and service.

> An American Ethos President must not belong to nor take special interest or political party money and owe no allegiance to these groups.

> An American Ethos President must bring all aspects of American political beliefs into the administration—not just democrat and republican but all interests and all ideologies that are interested in working together.

> An American Ethos President must be a pragmatic activist that is proactive and responsive to the needs of the American citizenry.

An American Ethos President must be available and answerable to the questions of the American people through weekly press conferences and open decision making processes.

An American Ethos Presidency must recognize the importance of civil liberties and the individual freedoms guaranteed in the Constitution and serve as the defender of these precious rights.

An American Ethos Presidency must utilize the power of the Office to work with private businesses to create jobs and secure an economic environment that cultivates growth.

An American Ethos Presidency must be committed to keeping our children's future at the forefront of the decision making process by building a culture of life long education.

An American Ethos Presidency must represent the American people by active participation in world community, engaging the world through mutually beneficial trade, cultural ties and defense treaties.

An American Ethos President must head a strong military, defending the American homeland and its citizenry from any threat, internal or external and never seeking permission from abroad before acting in our defense.

An American Ethos President must take positions that benefit all Americans—positions that are difficult yet necessary, progressive positions that utilize the best aspects of right and left, positions that are long term investments into America.

An American Ethos Presidency must be committed to bringing us together by creating and cultivating an American Ethos. By facilitating progress and encouraging all sides to work together to achieve the things we agree upon, an American Ethos Presidency will build a foundation for our future.

◆   ◆   ◆

I am an American. I am not a liberal and not a conservative. I am not a Republican and not a Democrat. I refuse to be subdivided and placed into an easily manipulated group. I am simply and proudly, an American. I have my own religion, my own values and my own outlook on the world. I am proud of our nation, our people and our accomplishments, but I do not believe we can rely on our past to ensure our present or our future. I cherish my freedoms and my country and I want to preserve my country and my freedoms for my children and their children. I know that my country, my fellow citizens and our common future are my responsibility.

As Americans, we must decide what kind of country we are going to have going forward. We must make decisions now that will shape our common future. As Americans, we must understand that we cannot expect our country as we know it to survive if we do not act now to preserve, protect and defend all that we collectively value and cherish. The future of our country is at stake and this is our shared responsibility.

Our future demands that we look at Americans as a whole group, not a collection of competing minorities fighting with each other, achieving nothing. We don't need morality and values as judged by the few. We need standards and ideals as necessitated by all. When we can view ourselves as Americans, with a common history and a common future, we can begin to break to hold of partisanship and regionalism and regain our power and ownership. The America I believe in deserves no less.

As Americans, we have a unique opportunity to live in the greatest country in the world simply because we have the power to change the system and make it work better. We must unite and utilize our democratic power—we must prioritize our goals, tackle issues of common necessity and build our national unity. We must depose the special interests and partisan extremists. We must elect rational, progressive leaders who will bring us together as Americans. We must refocus our collective efforts toward things we can agree are mutually important to us as Americans. When we do this, we can change the system. We can regain our national identity and cultivate a spirit of unanimity as Americans, regardless of our political, ideological, ethnic or religious background. We must become true owner-operators of our nation and our future.

We owe it to ourselves as Americans and our common American future to rebuild trust and respect in each other. When we do, we can reclaim ownership of our nation and take our place in history as Americans who were asked to defend our nation and who responded with unity, progressivism and idealism.

This is Our American Ethos.

978-0-595-36725-2
0-595-36725-9